W9-AZG-298

100th DAY

A SPOT-IT CHALLENGE

by Sarah L. Schuette

CAPSTONE PRESS
a capstone imprint

A+ Books are published by Capstone Press,
1710 Roe Crest Drive, North Mankato, Minnesota 56003.
www.capstonepub.com

Books published by Capstone Press are manufactured with paper
containing at least 10 percent post-consumer waste.

Library of Congress Cataloging-in-Publication Data
Schuette, Sarah, L., 1976–
100th Day: A Spot-It Challenge / by Sarah L. Schuette
p. cm (A+ Books. Spot it.)
Summary: "Simple Text invites the reader to find items hidden in 100th-day-of-school-themed
    photographs"—Provided by publisher.
ISBN 978-1-4296-7559-8 (library binding)
1. Picture puzzles—juvenile literature. I. Title. II. Series.
GV1507.P47 A15 2012
793.73—dc22   2011041601

Credits

Shelly Lyons, editor; Ted Williams, designer; Laura Manthe, production specialist;
    Sarah Schuette, photo stylist; Marcy Morin, photo scheduler; Eliza Cate Lynard,
    photo assistant

Photo Credits

All photos by Capstone Studio: Karon Dubke, except: Shutterstock: Gregory Dunn, paper texture,
trubach, title texture

The author dedicates this book to her cousin Elizabeth Schmidt.

Note to Parents, Teachers, and Librarians

Spot It is an interactive series that supports literacy development and reading enjoyment.
Readers utilize visual discrimination skills to find objects among fun-to-peruse photographs
with busy backgrounds. Readers also build vocabulary through them
793.atic groupings, develop
visual memory ability through repeated readings, and improve strategic and associative
thinking skills by experimenting with different visual search methods.

Printed in the United States of America in North Mankato, Minnesota.
052012   006725R

Table of Contents

100 Miles

Can you spot ...

- a top hat?
- a mitten?
- a watermelon?
- a cowboy boot?
- a comb?
- French fries?

5

Legend

al Capital
an 1 Million
) to 1 Million
) to 500,00
to 100 000
00
---- State Boundaries
Interstate Highway
Major Rivers
Dams
Lakes
Mountain Peaks
ft.(feet) m(meter)
National Parks

100 Feet

Can you spot ...

- a tomato?
- an anchor?
- a calculator?
- a screwdriver?
- a checker?
- a cookie cutter?

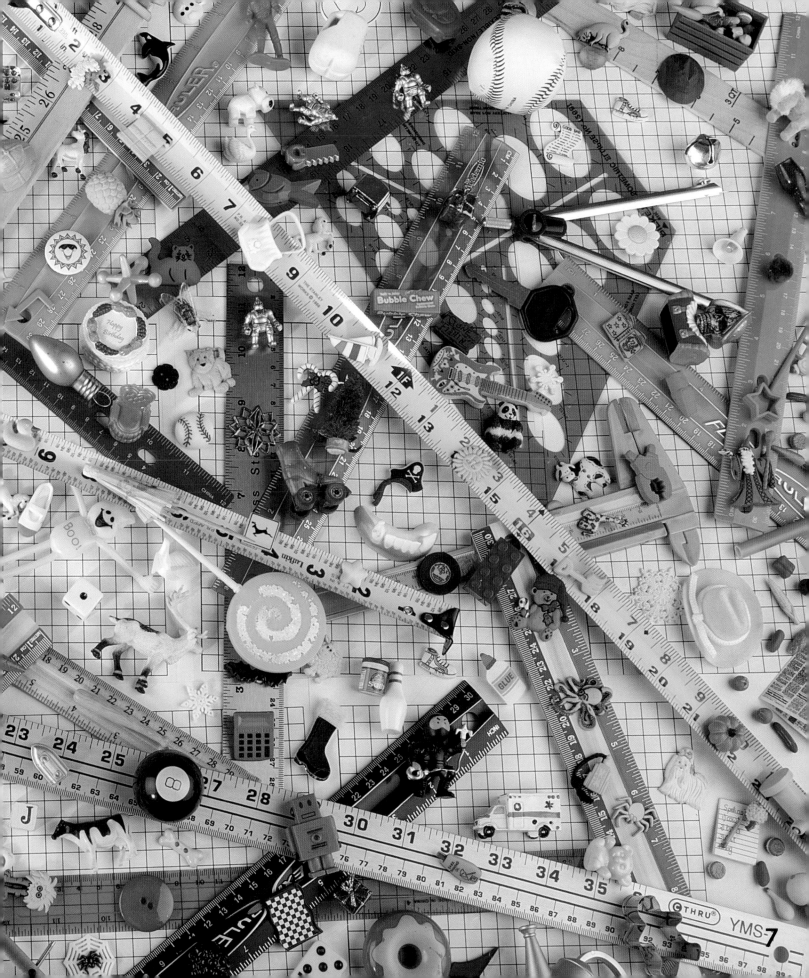

100 Dollars

Can you spot ...

- an ice-cream bar?
- a flip flop?
- a flashlight?
- two packs of gum?
- a plastic milk jug?
- a jet plane?

100 Dots

Can you spot ...
- a toaster?
- a trumpet?
- a unicorn?
- a piano?
- two black cats?
- a skateboard?

10

100 Pages

Can you spot ...

- a baby bottle?
- a microphone?
- a gingerbread woman?
- a newspaper?
- a nest?
- a bow and arrow?

100 Good Deeds

Can you spot ...

- a crescent moon?
- a dolphin?
- a ladder?
- two purses?
- a rocking horse?
- a watering can?

14

100 Words

Can you spot …
- a lasso?
- a donut?
- a rabbit?
- a plane?
- a scissors?
- a helicopter?

100 Fish

Can you spot ...
- a gold coin?
- a magic marker?
- two sharks?
- a parrot?
- a pinecone?
- a bowling pin?

18

100 Colors

Can you spot ...

- a pitchfork?
- two traffic cones?
- a motorcycle?
- a whistle?
- a castle?
- a ghost?

21

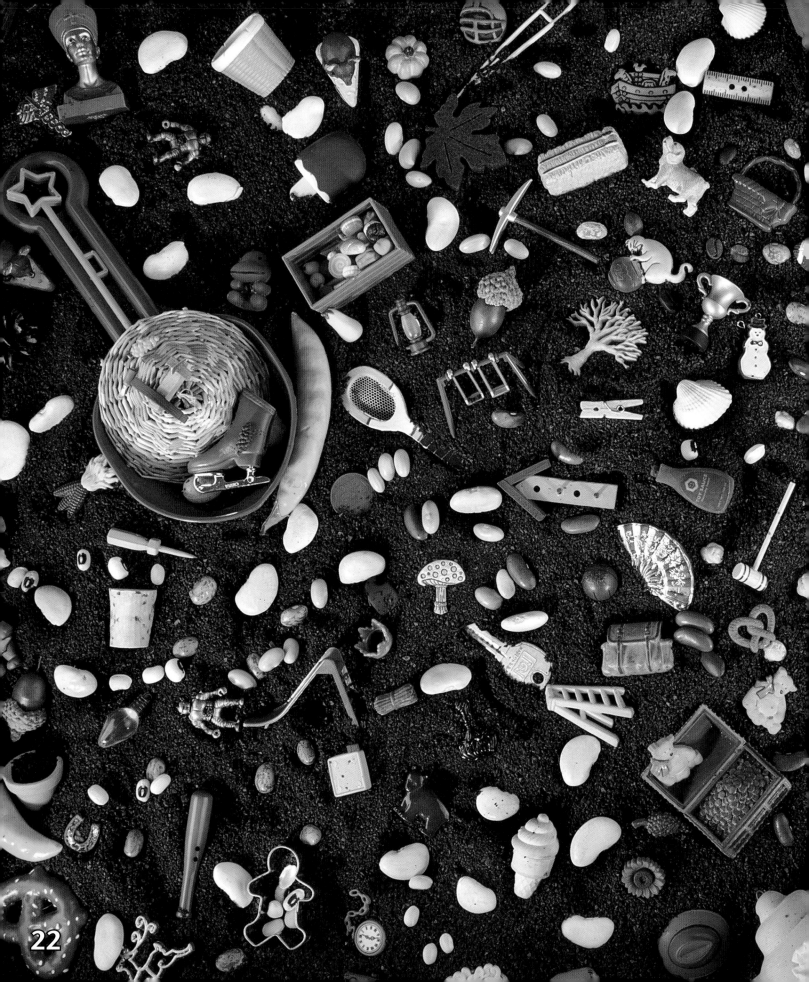

100 Beans

Can you spot …

- two sandwiches?
- a swing set?
- a mushroom?
- a bone?
- a cactus?
- a music note?

100 Hellos

Can you spot ...

- a sheep?
- a poodle?
- an otter?
- a zebra?
- two donkeys?
- a clothespin?

100 Wheels

Can you spot ...

- a toilet?
- a pea pod?
- a seashell?
- a football helmet?
- a panda?
- two astronauts?

Spot Even More!

100 Miles

Try to find a canteen, a gift bag, a pair of ballet slippers, and a sea lion. How about 100 red tacks?

100 Feet

Try to spot an ice-cream cone, a first aid kit, a pirate hat, a swan, and a deer on a sign.

100 Dollars

Find two bells, a rooster, a roll of toilet paper, a birthday candle, and a head of lettuce. Can you count 100 coins?

100 Dots

Try to find a fishing pole, two candy canes, two spiders, two buttons, and an antique sewing machine.

100 Pages

See if you can spot a birthday cake, a toothpaste tube, two chairs, and the number 100?

100 Good Deeds

Check for two pairs of sunglasses, a walrus, two snorkels, and a scarecrow.

100 Words

Look for underpants, a robot, a bunch of grapes, and three frogs. Do you see a number one and two zeros?

16

100 Fish

Now spot a treasure chest, a cob of corn, a caterpillar, and a sea turtle. Can you count 100 bobbers?

18

100 Colors

This time find a tombstone, two babies, the letter "J", and a strawberry. Try to count at least 100 crayons.

20

100 Beans

See if you can find a soda can, a band aid, two horseshoes, a cork, and a pencil. Count at least 100 beans.

22

100 Hellos

Now look for the number 100, two mittens, two pumpkins, a baseball bat, and two keys.

24

100 Wheels

See if you can spot a paw print, three school buses, two checkers, and a fish. Do you see 100 wheels?

26

Extreme Spot-It Challenge

Just can't get enough Spot-It action?
Here's an extra challenge. Try to spot:

- a cooking pot
- a witch hat
- a jack
- a palm tree
- a lion
- a donkey
- two elephants
- a whisk
- a Christmas stocking
- a nickel
- a pair of eyeglasses
- an umbrella
- an octopus
- a football jersey
- an acorn
- two bunches of cherries
- two cats

Read More

Bruning, Matt. *Zoo Picture Puzzles.* Look, Look Again. Mankato, Minn.: Capstone Press, 2010.

Chedru, Delphine. *Spot It Again!: Find More Hidden Creatures.* New York: Abrams Books for Young Readers, 2011.

Schuette, Sarah L. *Season Search: A Spot-It Challenge.* Spot It. Mankato, Minn.: Capstone Press, 2011.

Internet Sites

FactHound offers a safe, fun way to find Internet sites related to this book. All of the sites on FactHound have been researched by our staff.

Here's all you do:

Visit *www.facthound.com*

Type in this code: **9781429675598**

Super-cool stuff!

Check out projects, games and lots more at
www.capstonekids.com